The Precious Gift

**Written and Illustrated
by**

Sandra C. Saenz

AuthorHouse™
1663 Liberty Drive
Bloomington, IN 47403
www.authorhouse.com
Phone: 833-262-8899

Because of the dynamic nature of the Internet, any web addresses or links contained in this book may have changed
since publication and may no longer be valid. The views expressed in this work are solely those of the author and do not
necessarily reflect the views of the publisher, and the publisher hereby disclaims any responsibility for them.

Any people depicted in stock imagery provided by Getty Images are models,
and such images are being used for illustrative purposes only.
Certain stock imagery © Getty Images.

This book is printed on acid-free paper.

ISBN: 978-1-4567-4708-4 (sc)
ISBN: 978-1-4817-1518-8 (e)

Library of Congress Control Number: 2011903789

Print information available on the last page.

Published by AuthorHouse 01/29/2022

authorHOUSE®

We waited patiently for them to tell us our precious gift was on the way.

But the doctors made us sad with the news
they gave us that day.

"For you see," the doctors said, "your baby boy perfect will not be. Maybe his birth was not meant to be."

So we prayed and thanked the Lord. We remembered that the Lord is faithful, the Lord is true. It does not matter what may come our way, He will always come through.

The day our baby boy was born, the tubes and machines could not hide the joy we felt inside.

We looked through the Bible for the perfect name, one that no one else would find. So we named our baby Lot, the perfect name for a boy who was unique and kind.

The doctors always said, "Your baby is too sick and this hospital he will never leave. Maybe his life was just not meant to be."

So we prayed and thanked the Lord. We remembered that the Lord is faithful, the Lord is true. It does not matter what may come our way, He will always come through.

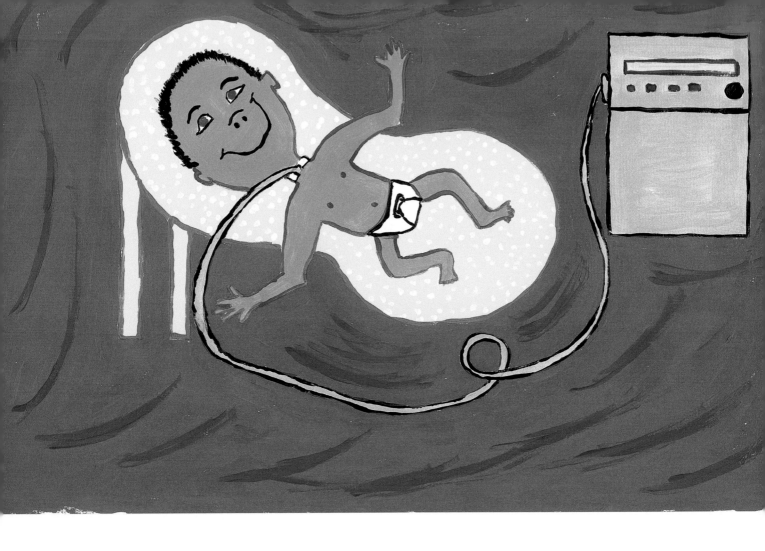

After six long months, Lot finally came home.

He grew.

and he grew,

and he grew.

"What's this? This child is doing so well!"
The doctors said, as they scratched their
heads. "Maybe his life was meant to be."

So we praised and thanked the Lord! We remembered that the Lord is faithful, the Lord is true. It does not matter what may come our way, He will always come through!!

Printed in the United States
by Baker & Taylor Publisher Services